I LOVE YC
DAD

BY IRIS HISKEY ARNO
ILLUSTRATED BY JOAN HOLUB

Troll

For some wonderful dads—my father, Clarence,
my father-in-law, Harold, and my husband, Peter
—I.H.A.

For Wally Wren, with love
—J.H.

I LOVE YOU, DAD

When Dad and I go fishing,
The water looks so cool.
My daddy says he wonders
What fishes learn in school.

Our ears are full of bird songs,
Our backs warmed by the sun.
And whether we catch fish or not,
My dad and I have fun!

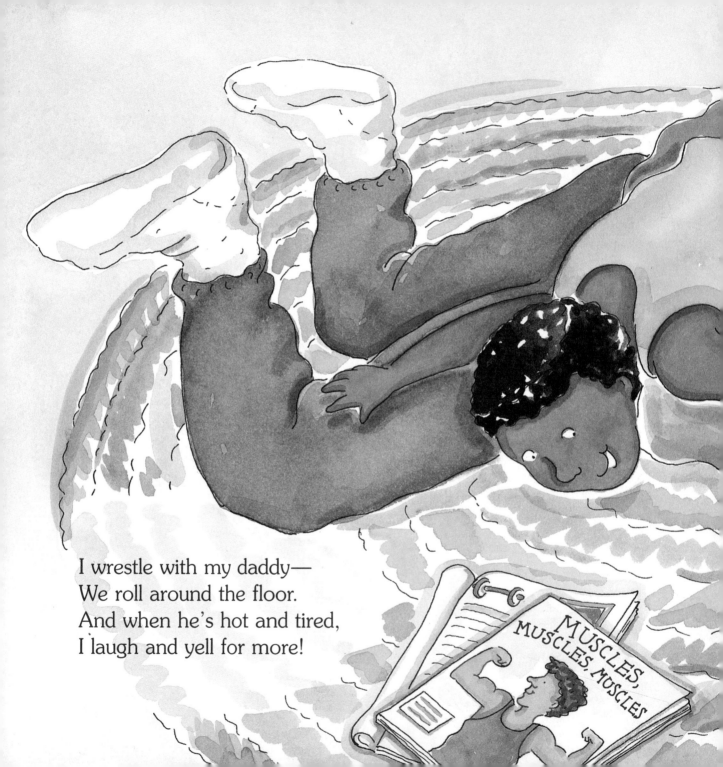

I wrestle with my daddy—
We roll around the floor.
And when he's hot and tired,
I laugh and yell for more!

His arms have such big muscles,
They bulge out of his shirt.
But though we always huff and puff,
I know I won't get hurt.

My dad and I love cooking;
We make the greatest stuff.
We fill our plates with piles of food
Till Mama cries, "Enough!"

We like to chop the carrots,
But onions make us cry.
We mix and beat and knead and bake—
Because we're chefs, that's why!

My dad throws me a fastball;
I take a mighty swing.
I hear the crack as bat slams ball—
It makes my eardrums ring.

Fast pitching used to scare me;
The ball might hit me—*whack!*
But now my dad has taught me how
To give that ball a smack!

We're happy in the garden,
Just digging in the dirt.
We find some worms and beetles
That we would never hurt.

We weed around our seedlings
And smell a dark red rose,
And if I say I'm getting bored,
Dad sprays me with the hose!

My dad and I play checkers,
And sometimes we play chess,
And cards and jacks and pick-up sticks—
We make a great big mess.

My dad says I'm a winner.
Though I don't always win,
I try to be a good sport
So I'll be just like him.

My dad and I love reading.
We choose some books each night
And read our favorite stories
Till Mom turns out the light.

And when a story's scary,
I snuggle close to Dad.
Then other times we start to cry
Because our book is sad.

We love to have big snow fights
In winters cold and white.
When Dad and I build snow forts,
I want to play all night.

The snowballs fly above us.
We scream and run around.
And when I sneak up on my dad,
My feet don't make a sound.

My dad and I play music;
We sing and dance about.
And when we get excited,
We like to whoop and shout!

Sometimes we play piano,
Sometimes we play guitars.
At night we sit out on the porch
And sing to all the stars.

My dad and I love flashlights.
We run around at night
And try to tag each other
With yellow beams of light.

The darkness used to scare me,
But now I have no fear.
Hey, what was that?
  Did you hear that?
Hey, Dad, come over here!

My daddy's metal toolbox
Is full of nifty things,
Like screwdrivers and hammers
And tape measures and springs.

He teaches me to use them
To fix whatever breaks
And doesn't even get too mad
If I make some mistakes!

I turn on the computer.
"Hey, Daddy, want to play?"
And even when he's tired,
My dad will say, "Okay!"

He really tries his hardest
To get the highest score.
But I'm a whiz—I can't be beat—
So my score's always more!

When he's away on business,
I really miss my dad.
He says he'll bring me souvenirs,
But I am still so sad.

I feel a little better
When the phone begins to ring.

I know it's Daddy calling me—
I wonder what he'll bring?

My dad and I make puppets.
We love to put on shows.
We make their faces and their hair
And decorate their clothes.

They talk in funny voices
And sometimes scream and fight.
We laugh so hard when Mom runs in
To make sure we're all right!

A dad is often busy,
With lots of work to do.
But there are always moments
That he'll save just for you.

The world is full of treasures,
With things to make you glad.
And someone wants to share them.
Guess who? Of course—your dad!